Monday Jan 10

The Church provided me with a great sendoff. I am very grateful to all of those involved. The special efforts of Rev W Seeley, Deacon Chapman, Deaconess Iura Smith are noted.

The packing is a hore and a chore! Janie has advised me on a number of things that I need to get out she right! The Ironomydium and Pepto Bismol are essential.

5:30 A.M.
Well, the time has not arrived but I'm sure it drops... in here it is 5:35.
The siren talks about the amount of traffic now on I 93. That was going to be only the beginning of the troubles for the day. The crowd at TWA was tremendous. Because of so many flights cancelled over the weekend a good number of people were trying to get on flight #36

PAUSE

FADE TO
BLACK

LIGHTS UP

ACTION

June 20, 1997 - Friday

There was a steady stream of ... cops -

FADL TO Black

1/12/94 - Wednesday
Left Netanya - went to Caesarea
Home of Philip - Jesus asked a
question
Caesarea was great on Sea
Mt Carmel - Down to
Armageddon - For Tunnel

Saw the Valley of JEZREEL - awesome
We traveled to Nazareth and went to
the Church of the Annunciation. The
beauty of the art work is breathtaking.
Rev. Badie & I left the group
to go back to the bus. We stopped
& tried on a couple of Vestments. We
also saw a beautiful item piece from
Russia. It depicts Jesus in Black.

We left Nazareth - By the way this is
a rough looking city - approx 60,000 people.
Badie reminded me of the saying -
Can any good thing come out of Nazareth?
I may have tried to snatch my
sermon.

1/13/94
We saw the Mt. of Beatitudes & it was very moving. The guide did a good job directing us to pray & meditate on Jesus. This is the believed to be site. The German Benedictine Order built a church at that site. Rev Beck of San Diego helped lead us in Devotion.

Tired, because Ev Ladies and I woke up in the early a.m. In fact this is partly me just by going writing now — the same thing has happened.

We ate at PETER Fish Restaurant. The "catch" was not very good but Wayne Fadie and I met a woman from South Carolina. She was a person with a Study Group in The Holy Land for 3-4 Weeks.

1/19 – I have not been able to write as I hoped. Most of the following are reflections as I sit on this 747 airline flight. I'm happy to be going home now. I know that there are many challenges awaiting me, but I'm really blessed. I'm blessed to have the kind of personality that God gave me. I see the trouble that Wayne is getting and I believe that I get more support because of my personality. That does not make me better, only more humble. This does not make me right but it allows others to "fill in" and hence it changes jobs. Sometimes it causes me trouble but at the present it has become a blessing.

I feel for Wayne. Valerie should have not scarred as much had she as she has. Yet maybe it will help him to leave. In fact any decisions are more complicated than this.

God, I've been to Jerusalem! and Rome! This kind of travel was well overdue. I believe that I will push the leave soon. The economic question will remain, but I will by the spirit Jamie & Jessen for the Ohio or Atlanta. I proceed with trembling and fear.

I plan to travel more. This was very relaxing. I'd like to move around above or with Jamie. Dear God I need your direction!

The Spirit was high in the ride to Jerusalem. The mountains were amazing. Rev. Horvatich's singing of the amazing Grace by the young man were moving. I was also moved by the manger in Bethlehem & the Brasque on Temple mount.

$1,000 of Spending Money is a good amount for both trips. If Janie had been with me we'd probably done better, I'm not a good tradesperson. Wayne did a great job.

Room, I really enjoyed the roomy truck. There are a lot of themes and the food was not as good as I hoped, but... Rose! I want the king Janie bed.

Friday June 20, 1997

Andover, MA - Why to Saudiarabi

There was a steady stream of sickly, sorrowful looking people in Quincy today. I never noticed that so many people with maladies came into that building. It is only by being still did I notice and see those with impairment around me. In the stillness of these precious moments I saw a new world. A world heretofore out of my consciousness. How could that be? How could I not see those so like me? Halted, Lame, Deaf, Mute, Blind, unable — How could I fail to see them?